Lots of players also sign up to Roblox Studio so that they can start making their own video games.

This is a great way to show off your creative skills and even acts as an introduction to basic coding. What kind of amazing video game ideas do you have?

If you're a truly massive fan of Roblox, there is also tons of cool merch that you can pick up.

There's a huge selection of T-shirts, books and action figures to get that feature your favourite Roblox characters. Impress your mates with your collection!

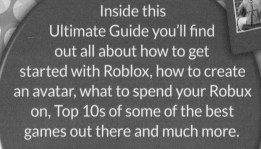

2020 was a massive year for Roblox.

More people started creating and playing games than ever before and there were all kinds of fun virtual events, from concerts and awards shows to competitions and treasure hunts. But 2021 will be even bigger!

Inside this Ultimate Guide you'll find out all about how to get started with Roblox, how to create an avatar, what to spend your Robux on, Top 10s of some of the best games out there and much more.

Get ready to step into a universe of gaming!

HOW TO PLAY

If you're new to the world of Roblox, you might not be too sure how to get started. Well, it couldn't be easier!

No matter if you're playing on a PC, console, mobile or even a VR device, here are some handy hints to help you dive in.

Roblox is free to play regardless of what device you're using, so it's really simple to begin.

Once you've chosen which platform to play on, you'll need to create a player profile and character (or avatar). You can choose from a selection of different faces, body parts, clothing and accessories to get the look you're after.

If you can't find any items that you want, then head on over to the Avatar Shop (see page 16).

Here you'll be able to browse a huge selection of clothes, gear and other cool stuff. Some of the items are free, but others you'll have to pay for. For those you'll need to start using the in-game currency, Robux.

There are a number of different ways to get hold of Robux (see page 26).

You can buy physical Robux Gift Cards and use the code on them to add amounts to your game or purchase Robux in the game itself. It's also possible to get Robux by signing up for Roblox Premium or by making games and selling virtual items.

About | Creations

About

Currently Wearing

3D

Statistics

lace Visits
0

Item	Price	Item	Price	Item	Price
Shiny Teeth	35	Black and Red	90	Thick Rimmed Glasses 3.0	85
Stitchface	4,000	Shiny Reindeer Nose	25	Earring Hoops By Builder_Boy	50
Clean Shiny Spikes By Yourius	80	Happy	25	Diamond Stud Earrings By Builder_Boy	75

Bandage By WhoToTrus 50 — Black Headband By Geocentrisme 80
It's Go Time! 150 — Whistle 33
Slickfang 175 — Freckles 10

Get Robux to purchase upgrades for your avatar or buy special abilities in games. For more information on how to earn Robux, visit our Robux Help page. Purchase Roblox Premium to get more Robux for the same price. Roblox Premium is billed every month until cancelled. Learn more here.

	Buy Robux	Subscribe and get more!
	400	450/month
99	800	1,000/month
£18.49	1,700	2,200/month
Value Packs		
£46.49	4,500	

CONTENTS

STAYING SAFE ONLINE

It's always best to check with a parent or guardian before playing online with others.

SPENDING ROBUX

Buying items in the game costs Robux, so check with an adult first before purchasing content.

Brother

Published 2021.
Little Brother Books Ltd, Ground Floor, 23 Southernhay East, Exeter, Devon EX1 1QL
books@littlebrotherbooks.co.uk | www.littlebrotherbooks.co.uk
Printed in Turkey.
The Little Brother Books trademarks, logos, email and website addresses and the GamesWarrior logo and imprint are sole and exclusive properties of Little Brother Books Limited.

WELCOME TO THE WORLD OF... ROBLOX!

As one of the most popular online multiplayer experiences in the world, Roblox is absolutely huge. With over 150 million players now signed up to the game, it's as big a success today as it was when it launched over 10 years ago!

You're never too far away from fun, adventure and excitement in Roblox as there are so many totally awesome games to play.

From simulations, sports and action titles to RPGs, platformers and shooters, there's something for everyone.

One of the many great things about Roblox is that almost everything on the platform is free, including games and avatar items.

If you want to take things to the next level you can always pay for stuff with Robux for even more possibilities.

Project Bronze: Reborn
85% 7.6K

[UPDATE 1]Grand Piece
94% 3.1K

Warrior Cats: Ultimate Edition
94% 744

Electric State DarkRP(Beta)
84% 1.2K

Shindo Life
94% 46.3K

(Route 8) Loomian Legacy
92% 3.9K

Bee Swarm Simulator
94% 42.8K

[MUTA...]
84%

Recommended For You

Adopt Me!
84% 377.5K

Brookhaven RP
90% 269.8K

[UPDATE 13] Blox Fruits
91% 61.1K

All Star Tower Defense
93% 64.7K

Shindo Life
94% 46.3K

Bee Swarm Simulator
94% 42.8K

Murder Mystery
92% 68.8K

Up-and-Coming

*NEW] Bank ...oon!
3.1K

[LA... Soi...

Once you're happy with the way your avatar appears, you can start playing games. Click on the Games link and you'll be presented with a number of different titles in various categories.

From RPGs, Adventure and Fighting to Obby, Simulator and Tycoon, there really is something for everyone!

Click on a game you like the look of to find out more about it. There's a description for the game, information on how many people are playing it, how many visits it's had and the maximum number of players allowed.

Most games are free to play, but as with items from the Shop, Robux may be required to buy others.

ADVERTISEMENT

ADOPT ME!

Adopt Me!
By DreamCraft

▶

Favorite Follow 3M+ 635K+

About   Store   Servers

Description

Raise and dress cute pets, decorate your house, and play with friends in the magical, family-friendly world of Adopt Me! on Roblox!

We've been cold long enough, bye bye winter!
New updates coming soon!
Check our Twitter for news and competitions!
New chances to win pets every week!

Playing Roblox online is a massively fun multiplayer experience and you'll often team up with and compete against people from around the world.

Most games have the option for you to set up private servers (sometimes with a Robux fee) so that you can play games in peace with just your friends.

Once you've picked a game to play, use the controls on your chosen platform to move around, look around and interact.

You can also talk to other players in-game using the Chat & Play function. Get ready to explore a universe of amazing games as you prepare to discover just how much fun Roblox can be!

WHAT'S NEW IN ROBLOX

There's always something fun going on in the Roblox universe! From special events and exclusives to movie tie-ins and coding challenges, this is one game that never stands still. How many of these do you know about?

150 MILLION PLAYERS

There are lots of Roblox players all over the world. In fact there are more than 150 million of them! The game smashed its previous record in the summer of 2020 as lots more players spent time online trying out all sorts of Roblox titles.

READY PLAYER TWO TREASURE HUNT

The original event attracted over 13 million players, but the Ready Player Two Treasure Hunt smashed that by nearly double! Complete the seven levels to find all relics, solve puzzles, win a grand prize and even bag some exclusive avatar items.

GUCCI SNEAKER GARAGE

If you like wearing the latest super-hot footwear, then check out the GUCCI Sneaker Garage! The world's biggest fashion label added a section to its mobile app that lets you create a pair of virtual shoes for your Roblox avatar. So cool!

HALLOWEEN FUN

Lots of video games have Halloween-themed events, but Roblox does it in spooky style! In 2020 one of Roblox's education partners, iD Tech, hosted an awesome Halloween Block Party. The event included a virtual trick or treat challenge and more!

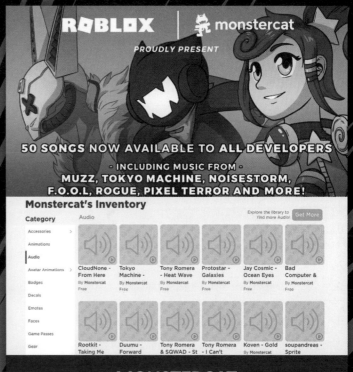

MONSTERCAT

In July, 2020 independent electronic label Monstercat joined forces with Roblox to offer creators 51 tracks of cool music for free! Players can use these tunes in their own games and there are even more tracks on the way.

SUMMER CODING CHALLENGE

Lots of Roblox players have taken the leap and started making their own games. In 2020 Roblox launched the Build It Play It summer coding challenge to show kids and teens how to build game with custom animations. There were even special rewards!

WONDER WOMAN EVENT

To celebrate the launch of the Wonder Woman 1984 movie, Warner Bros. and DC teamed up with Roblox to launch an awesome game. Wonder Woman: The Themyscira Experience had mini-games, quests and even exclusive avatar items to purchase.

TOP 10 RPGs

Did you know that role playing games are some of the most popular titles on Roblox? There are plenty to choose from, so check out our list of the best RPGs that you have to start playing!

TELEPORT

#10 KINGDOM LIFE II

Lv. 4   Lv. 3

ROBLOX FACT:
Kingdom Life II has been played by gamers over 15 million times!

Creator: Boopbot
Release Date: April 2009

Step into a Medieval fantasy world filled with excitement and adventure. In this RPG players can take on one of a number of customisable roles including elves, wizards, dragons, giants fairies and even animals. They then have to explore an ancient castle and surrounding areas, battling enemies and levelling up their characters.

There are two game modes in Kingdom Life II: Player versus player (pvp) and role-playing. In pvp you take on others in epic combat using different weapons until only one of you is left standing. In role-playing you can't kill other players, but you can't be killed either. Handy for long adventuring sessions!

RUMBLE QUEST

#9

Creator: Rumble Studios
Release Date: November 2019

Rumble Quest is epic questing at its very best. In this game players take on a number of tough challenges such as battling massive dragons and fighting evil bosses. By defeating enemies and completing quests, you'll earn lots of loot and can then use it to upgrade all of your character's equipment.

Explore a variety of locations such as underground realms, Medieval villages, jungle temples, ancient tombs and more areas. Hordes of enemies will need to be beaten to give you loot to buy equipment, cosmetics, weapons, armour and abilities. Get questing!

ROBLOX FACT:
The max level that players can reach in Rumble Quest is level 290!

#8

ROBLOX HIGH SCHOOL 2

Creator: Cinder Studio
Release Date: July 2018

If you were a fan of the original game, then you'll want to check out the sequel, Roblox High School 2! This time around players get to enter an all-new school environment and try out lots of new mini games to boost their grades. By exploring the school you'll encounter new friends and discover cool secrets.

Players can customise their avatars with a variety of skins, buy awesome vehicles, tasty food and custom music IDs. The forthcoming Graduation Update arriving in 2021 will add another new map to the game, plus fan-requested features from the original Roblox High School game. Study hard and become the best in your class!

ROBLOX FACT:
Roblox High School 2 used to cost 25 Robux, but is now free-to-play!

#7

DUNGEON QUEST

Creator: vCaffy
Release Date: July 2018

The aim of the game is to successfully make your way through a series of 11 gloomy dungeons, battling wave after wave of enemies. Players can go solo or team up with others to beat enemies, level up and grab lots a precious items.

At the end of each dungeon is a fearsome boss to fight. These battles can be quite tricky, so it's a good idea to go into them with the best gear, weapons and abilities as possible. Items have different colours to show rarity, with Legendary being orange. Learn boss patterns and the layouts of dungeons for the best chance of survival.

ROBLOX FACT:
Upgrading just one aspect of your character in the game is known as Minmaxing!

#6

HERO HAVOC SIMULATOR

Hero Havoc Simulator transports players to a strange world full of evil creatures and high adventure. The land is being threatened by the monstrous Demon King and it's up to you to save the day! The only way to do this is team up with other players to take on the forces of darkness.

Exploring the world and completing quests leads to battles with monsters. Players will need to make sure they have the best weapons, items and abilities in order to take down their enemies. You can also customise your character with different skins to create the perfect RPG adventurer.

ROBLOX FACT:
Players with Roblox Premium can get free bonus gems for every hour they play!

Creator: wish_z
Release Date: January 2019

#5

WELCOME TO BLOXBURG

ROBLOX FACT: Welcome to Bloxburg won best Mobile game of the year in the 7th Annual Bloxy Awards!

A truly epic game that's had over three billion visits since it launched, Welcome to Bloxburg is a life-simulation with millions of fans worldwide. Players get to build their own houses using different materials, travel around the city in cool vehicles, hang out with their mates and do all kinds of jobs. You can also do jobs for money, which can then be used to buy more items, clothes and stuff – just like in real life!

Creator: Coeptus
Release Date: November 2014

Players can spend their Robux on Gamespasses that allow access to additional skills and perks to earn you more money. If you manage to reach level 50 in a job, you'll be given the 'Excellence Award' to show off to your friends. The game is packed with hours of activities to try and no two days in Bloxburg are ever the same!

#4 WORK AT A PIZZA PLACE

Creator: Cinder Studio
Release Date: July 2018

ROBLOX FACT: Work at a Pizza Place was the first Roblox game to get 100 million visits!

Who doesn't love pizza? In this fantastic job simulation game, players become a worker at a pizza restaurant and take on a number of roles in order to earn cash. Moneyz (coins) can then be used to upgrade and decorate your house and to buy cool gear. When you run out of cash, you'll need to work again to earn more!

Recent additions to the game have included pets for players to look after and stickers that can be used to customise your house. Players should also teleport over to Party Island and throw a fun bash for all their friends and dance the night away. Check out the Double Time event in the game, where orders turn into gold and rainbow pizzas!

Beach House Roleplay Retro

#3

ROBLOX FACT: Over 40 million players visited the original version of Beach House Roleplay Retro!

Creator: ak47master101
Release Date: September 2016

The original version of this game was created by DizzyPurple back in 2017, but was suspended as players kept spamming and destroying parts of it! This great remake of Beach House Roleplay Retro is just as good though and takes place in a cool holiday resort where up to 10 players can hang out and soak up the sunshine.

The world consists of a main hotel, with a pool area outside and a number of shops and external buildings to check out. Feel free to grab a sun lounger and chill by the pool or even take a stroll down the sandy beachfront. It's best to go inside the hotel first though and to chat to the receptionists before grabbing yourself a free room.

The shops have lots of fun stuff to buy from hats, ice creams and pets to clothes, tans and Ro-tocycles.

There are other vehicles dotted around the resort, so feel free to hop into any of them and take a quick drive. Players can buy items with gems and they'll earn one gem every 40 seconds. The longer you play, the more gems you'll get.

One of the really fun parts of Beach House Roleplay Retro is the ability to purchase pets. There are all kinds of cute companions to buy, so be sure to pick the one that's right for you. Once you've bought a pet it will follow you around and you can even buy special clothes for it from the shops or with a Gamepass using Robux.

HAIR SALON

ROTORCYCLE

#2

World // Zero

Creator: World // Zero
Release Date: January 2019

Easily one of the best RPGs available on Roblox, World // Zero has been visited by players over 80 million times! Prepare to head out on an epic multiplayer quest that will take you through numerous levels as you face tough challenges and enemies. You'll also need plenty of practice if you're going to take on many fearsome bosses!

Players can choose from one of three starter classes when they begin the game: Swordmaster, Mage and Defender. Each class has its own abilities and appearance, both of which can be tweaked as the game progresses. Collect tokens from quests and boss fights and you can unlock even more character classes.

Completing quests and battling foes will also reward you with gold and gems. These can then be spent on upgrading your character's gear, weapons and abilities. There are over 100 weapons to unlock in the game, so you'll need plenty of cash! Players can also collect and evolve their very own pets to accompany them on their journey.

With plenty of exploring, battling and grinding you'll eventually be able to take your character up to level 85, making them super-powerful. The game has also featured themed Battlepass packs which are available for a limited time. The Christmas pack included the tough Corrupted Claus Boss to beat!

ROBLOX FACT: World // Zero managed to win the 2019 Bloxy Award for Best Use of Tech!

#1

Adventure Up!

Creator: Read, set, play!
Release Date: May 2019

Fans of classic dungeon crawlers and MMORPGs will definitely want to check out Adventure Up! This is a very slick RPG that looks like the sort of a title a professional video game development studio would create. The game has had a lot of updates over the past few years that only help to improve and add to its awesomeness.

The scope of this game is absolutely huge. The levels are long and packed with all sorts of enemies and massive bosses to battle and there are plenty of quests to keep you playing for ages. Explore and conquer mysterious dungeons, craft unique special items and upgrade your weapons and armour to boost your abilities.

When the game begins players can choose from one of four professions to master. These are Alchemy, Crafting, Mining and Woodcutting. By fighting foes, crafting items and completing tasks your character will soon level up, allowing you to take on even bigger challenges. The more you do, the stronger your character becomes.

You can also customise the look of your character with a selection of various hairstyles, outfits, faces and more options. This is a great feature in the game, as it allows you to change your look to match your chosen profession. Items, equipment, tools and weapons all cost gold or gems, which can be found throughout the levels by battling enemies.

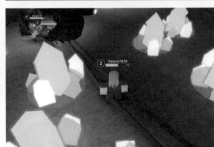

ROBLOX FACT: It's possible for up to 36 players to take part in an Adventure Up! quest together.

The main hub of the game is a town that contains different shops and merchants for players to explore. It's here that you can buy new items, upgrade equipment, purchase costumes and pick up a free Daily Reward. There's also a Time Trial to beat, Balloon Ride to go on and the main portal to teleport to the dungeons.

One of the other great things about the game is that players can explore the various worlds to build up their abilities or team up with other players. Tackling dungeons with a team of characters who also have different abilities is really fun and helps make short work of even the toughest of boss characters.

Head on over to the Adventure Up! Store and there are all sorts of goodies to buy with Robux. Gamepasses get you a special nametag, 25% extra experience, a 25% extra gem drop chance, extra boss loot, an extra life and much more. Splash out 100 Robux and you can even have your own private server for hosting games!

CUSTOMISE YOUR AVATAR

One of the best things about Roblox is you can change the look of your character (or avatar). Switch their face, hair, clothes, accessories and poses... the choice is endless and completely up to you!

This section looks a little different depending on whether you're playing on a PC, console or mobile, but it functions just the same. You can scroll through and select from lots of different options to allow you to change the look of your character until they appear exactly how you want them to.

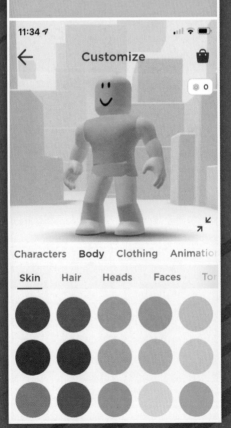

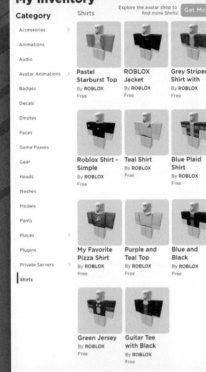

Did you know that your avatar in the game is also known as a Robloxian? This fun looking character is how you appear in a lot of Roblox games and it allows you to show off your style to other players. Your avatar is completely customisable and can be easily changed in the Avatar Editor.

There are a lot of free accessories to choose from to get you started, or you can check out the Avatar Shop and purchase more items using Robux (see page 26). Once you've chosen the items that you like, you can try them on your avatar, mixing and matching styles to get the perfect look.

Avatars used to look all blocky, as if they had just stepped out of Minecraft! As Roblox was updated, they began to look more human. When you first begin customising your avatar you may only swap out your character's hair and clothes, but before long you'll be updating your look almost every day!

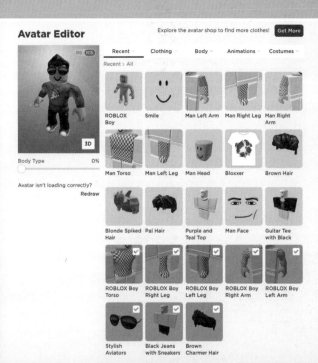

Avatar Editor
Explore the avatar shop to find more clothes! Get More

Recent | Clothing | Body | Animations | Costumes
Recent > All

R6 R15

Body Type 0%

Avatar isn't loading correctly?
Redraw

ROBLOX Boy | Smile | Man Left Arm | Man Right Leg | Man Right Arm
Man Torso | Man Left Leg | Man Head | Bloxxer | Brown Hair
Blonde Spiked Hair | Pal Hair | Purple and Teal Top | Man Face | Guitar Tee with Black
ROBLOX Boy Torso | ROBLOX Boy Right Leg | ROBLOX Boy Left Leg | ROBLOX Boy Right Arm | ROBLOX Boy Left Arm
Stylish Aviators | Black Jeans with Sneakers | Brown Charmer Hair

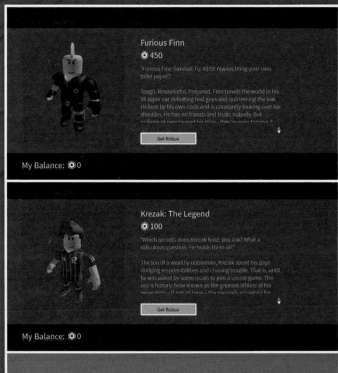

Furious Finn
⬡ 450

"Furious Finn Survival Tip #109: Always bring your own toilet paper."

Tough. Resourceful. Prepared. Finn travels the world in his V8 super car defeating bad guys and outrunning the law. He lives by his own code and is constantly looking over his shoulder. He has no friends and trusts nobody. But millions of people read his blog – they're even turning it

Get Robux

My Balance: ⬡ 0

Krezak: The Legend
⬡ 100

"Which records does Krezak hold, you ask? What a ridiculous question. He holds them all."

The son of a wealthy nobleman, Krezak spent his days dodging responsibilities and chasing trouble. That is, until he was asked by some locals to join a soccer game. The rest is history. Now known as the greatest athlete of his generation – if not all time – the people's adoration for

Get Robux

My Balance: ⬡ 0

Some versions of Roblox offer players ready-made avatars, so that they don't need to spend time creating their own. These avatars usually cost Robux, but are well worth it as they look fantastic. They also usually have a funny backstory attached to them, which tells you more about their character.

You can check out all of the items that you have for your avatar in your Inventory. This section of the game shows you all of the free and paid for accessories that you've collected and basically acts as a big wardrobe for you to choose items from. The more you get, the more options you'll have.

Category

Accessories > Hat
Explore the catalog to find more Accessories! Get More

Accessories
Animations
Audio
Avatar Animations >
Badges
Decals
Emotes
Faces
Game Passes
Gear
Heads
Meshes
Models
Pants
Places
Plugins
Shirts
T-Shirts

FabergEgg of the New | Binary Bunny Ears of | White Banded Red Top Hat | Eggveloper Egg of "X,Y,Z" | ##### ### ##### | Fluffy Black Bunny Hood
By ROBLOX Offsale | By ROBLOX Offsale | By ROBLOX Offsale | By ROBLOX Offsale | By Beeism ⬡ 200 | By Beeism ⬡ 150

Fuzzy Black Bear Hood | Fuzzy Polar Bear Hood | Chinese Tassels In | Lovely Blue Lace Bonnet | Lovely Black n White Lace | Lovely Lace Pink Bow
By Beeism ⬡ 150 | By Beeism ⬡ 150 | By OceanOrbs ⬡ 50 | By OceanOrbs ⬡ 100 | By OceanOrbs ⬡ 100 | By OceanOrbs ⬡ 100

Lovely Lace Pink Bonnet | Pastel Mermaid | Butterfly Antlers of | Knights of the Splintered | International Fedora - | Scoops Ahoy Hat
By OceanOrbs ⬡ 100 | By ROBLOX ⬡ 200 | By ROBLOX ⬡ 100 | By ROBLOX ⬡ 200 | By ROBLOX Free | By ROBLOX Offsale

Demogorgon Mask | Pepper Krinklesnaps - | Jester Equinox - Hat | Neapolitan Crown | Glorious Ram Horns | Brilliant Moon and Stars
By ROBLOX Offsale | By ROBLOX Offsale | By ROBLOX Offsale | By ROBLOX ⬡ 1,000 | By ROBLOX ⬡ 100 | By ROBLOX

11:33

Avatar

⬡ 0

As you can play Roblox almost anywhere, you can even edit your avatar on the go! Just grab the mobile version of the game, go into the Avatar Editor and make your selection. Once you've chosen your appearance, your avatar is saved and can be accessed on any platform that you like!

TOP 10 OBBY GAMES

If you're looking for fast-paced, crazy races over all kinds of challenging terrain, then Obby (or obstacle) games are for you! Here's our rundown of the Top 10 titles for you to tackle to become a true Roblox winner...

THE REALLY EASY OBBY!

#10

Creator: GFink
Release Date: August 2010

First up is one of the oldest (but best) Obby games to play. With over 300 million visits, The Really Easy Obby! Is up there with the most popular games on Roblox. Players have to try and beat 30 tough stages that feature a variety of obstacles to overcome. Run, balance, tiptoe, dodge and navigate through each level to earn badges.

Some of the stages are tough, so you'll need lots of practice to beat them all. The game includes a shop for players to spend Robux and coins on Gamepasses, special capes and cool trails. Dash over vanishing rainbow paths, leap over lava and avoid falling rocks to survive in one piece!

ROBLOX FACT:
Play the game with the volume cranked up to hear its cool soundtrack!

Creator: MysterOy
Release Date: December 2009

#9 ESCAPE THE BATHROOM

There are bunch of Escape the Bathroom obby titles on Roblox, but this is one of the best. Players have to use skill and timing to make their way over a giant bathroom full of obstacles, including navigating around someone sat on the toilet! One wrong step and you'll have to restart the section of the level where you left off.

Hazards to dodge in this game include dripping taps, leaking sewage pipes, floating shampoo bottles and prickly toothbrushes. Make it to the end and you're rewarded with some awesome skins, faces and trails to choose from. Play the level again with a trail and it's a lot easier!

ROBLOX FACT:
Successfully escape the bathroom to earn a special toilet badge!

#8 MEGA FUN OBBY

PLAY MY NEW CHRISTMAS OBBY!

Are you after a challenging obstacle game with a ton of levels? Then check out the 2305 stages in Mega Fun Obby! Not only are there plenty of tricky courses to try out, but most of them are can take quite a while to finish. Before you know it, you may discover you've been playing the game for a long time without a break.

The game also has over 261 badges for players to collect. Some of these require you to complete special challenges, while others are rewarded for just joining the game, every 10th stage finished and for smashing through the 1000th stage. How many can you collect?

ROBLOX FACT:
Mega Fun Obby gets updated every few days, so there are always new levels!

Creator: Bloxtun
Release Date: July 2009

#7 TOWER OF HELL

Creator: YXCeptional Studios
Release Date: June 2018

If ever a game was accurately named, it's Tower of Hell! In this challenging multiplayer obby title, players have to race to the top of a randomly generated tower to see who can make it first. There are no checkpoints to pass through, so make a mistake and you'll end up right back at the start.

The tower resets every eight minutes and a new round starts. If one player completes the tower, the timer resets and everything speeds up for the remaining players Experienced players can access the Pro Towers which have double the number of sections and two additional minutes to finish them.

ROBLOX FACT:
There are 226 sections in Tower of Hell including 16 super-secret sections!

#6 OBSTACLE PARADISE

Creator: I-C-T Studios
Release Date: January 2017

ROBLOX FACT:
Up to eight of your friends can take part on your obby creation at once!

Here's a fun obby game with a difference. In Obstacle Paradise players can build their very own obby courses and then race on them. You can buy all sorts of different building materials in the Store and combine them into whatever kind of level you like. Try out obstacles and hazards to see what works best and swap them for others.

As the game progresses your character earns money to spend on items. While waiting to get more cash, you can play on your friends' obbies to see how they create levels. Extras that can be purchased with Robux include a Double Jump, Checkpoints, Creative Mode and Unlimited Obby, which lets you place as many items as you like.

Be sure to join TycoonLab!

The LifeGuard has gone Mad! We must escape before he gets us!

Buy these boost to destroy your enemies along the way!

Creator: Tycoon Lab
Release Date: April 2020

ESCAPE THE EVIL WATERPARK OBBY!

#5

ROBLOX FACT:
Escape the Evil Waterpark Obby! Has been visited more than 9 million times!

Get ready for a parkour run that will push your skills to the limit! The lifeguard has gone completely crazy, so watch out for him as you try to make it out alive. There are lots of stages in Escape the Evil Waterpark Obby!, each with their own obstacles to navigate. With a bit of practice you should soon be blasting through each level in record time.

Extras in the Store include the Troll Pack (which lets you troll everyone in the level) and God Pack, which gets you a Flying Cloud and powerful God Staff. If a level is proving to be a bit too tough, it is possible to skip a few for free, but extra skips will cost Robux.

Quickly, Lets get past the shower room!

#4

Creator: crossbands!
Release Date: April 2020

ESCAPE MINIONS PARKOUR!

If you like those crazy Minions from the Despicable Me movies, then this obby is definitely for you! Find a way to make it through some long levels while dodging a number of tricky hazards. Up to 20 players can take part on an obby and you can even set up a private server to play games with just your friends.

At the start of a level you can choose to play as your own avatar or choose one of the other costumes on display. Making it through levels can take a while and you need to be careful not to get knocked off the edge of obstacles by other players. Make it to the end of the course to be rewarded with a special Minions surprise!

ROBLOX FACT:
If you're having trouble with a level, you can skip to the next one using Robux.

(ONLY R$30)

Baldi's Basics
#3 OBBY PARKOUR!

Creator: DevEnrique92000
Release Date: May 2020

Although there are a bunch of games on Roblox with a similar name, we think this version of Baldis Basics Obby Parkour Obby! is the best. The game has had over 8.6 million visits since it was created, proving to be extremely popular with gamers. Players have to navigate their way over obstacles and successfully escape Baldi's parkour stages.

Baldi is the strange giant figure seen in every level and there are lots of hazards to beat before you'll manage to make it safely past all of his challenges. As with all obbies, this game requires plenty of careful timing and coordination if you want to avoid falling and respawning. Also be sure to watch out for other players who may get in your way.

Up to 20 players can take part in a level at once, which can mean there's a lot of competition for first place. At the start of a level players can choose to tackle the course as their own avatar or select one of the alternative costumes on display. If a stage is too tough, players choose to pay Robux to skip it or go to the end of the game.

Levels can get very tough very quickly, but there's no timer so it's best not to rush your way through. Some of the obstacles you need to stand on are also very small, making accurate jumping essential. The shop has a few items to buy, but they don't really add to the game, so save your Robux for skips if you prefer.

ROBLOX FACT:
If you manage to make it through the whole game you'll get a secret surprise!

Welcome to Bloxburg

#2

ESCAPE BLOXBURG OBBY PARKOUR!

Creator: Parkour
Release Date: August 2020

ROBLOX FACT: Although only recently created, the game already has had over 1.4 million visits!

Welcome to Bloxburg is one of the most popular games on Roblox, but this obby lets you try and escape from it! There are 66 different sections of the course to blast through in this title, with up to 20 players competing against each other. Take on your mates to see who can be the Escape Bloxburg Obby Parkour! Champion!

Players start the game in a small Bloxburg house connected to the course. Walking through the door introduces you to all of the obstacles that lie ahead, stretching off into the distance. Hazards begin with quite simple challenges, but soon get a lot tougher. Make it over each part of the course to reach the safety of a spawn point.

If you fall off the edge of any section, you'll be transported back to the start of the section to try again. Be prepared, as this will happen a lot! As with other obbies, there will be competing players in the game, but don't let them distract you. If someone is on your section of the course, wait for them to go then follow when it's clear.

There's a special surprise waiting for you at the end of the game, but getting to it may take a while. The closer you get to the giant Bloxburg statue at the end, the tougher the challenges become. As with other obbies you can skip stages by paying with Robux or purchase an extra item that allows you to invite your friends.

#1 ESCAPE SANTA'S WORKSHOP OBBY!

Creator: Mega Obbies
Release Date: June 2020

With this great game, you can experience Christmas every single day of the year! In Escape Santa's Workshop Obby you have to make it safely out of the jolly one's workshop by dodging all sorts of hazards across 29 stages. Up to 10 players can all take part in a race against each other, so see if you can be the fastest.

At the start of the game players can either select which world they'd like to work their way through, or go to the main doors of Santa's workshop. Outside the doors is a friendly elf who also appears at the beginning of a level and explains what's going on. Head inside and great ready for some tough obby action!

The stages start off quite easy, but soon get a lot tougher. A variety of obstacles have to be beaten, from barriers, drops and laser grids to conveyor belts, pink slime and thin beams. You won't be racing against the clock in this game, so take your time to make it through each stage in one piece. Fall or hit an obstacle and you go back to the last checkpoint.

ROBLOX FACT:
With over 33 million visits in less than a year, this is one very popular obby!

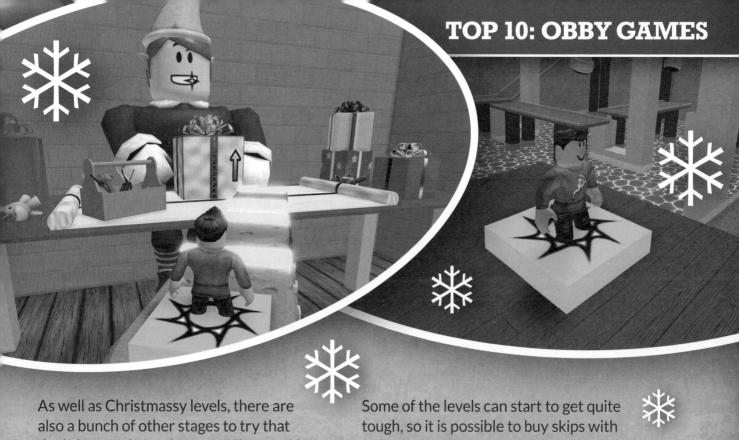

As well as Christmassy levels, there are also a bunch of other stages to try that don't feature Santa, but are still tons of fun to blast through. Check out Ride a Toilet, Escape the Barbershop, Escape School and Escape the Castle of Doom for even more challenges. Some of them can be a little gross, so pick your stage carefully!

One of the other great things about Escape Santa's Workshop Obby is the music. Each level has some really fantastic tunes and some Christmas-themed jingles add to the holiday feeling. Even if you're finding it tough to tackle a particular challenge, you won't be able to stop feeling like it's the 25th of December every time you play.

Some of the levels can start to get quite tough, so it is possible to buy skips with Robux to get you passed the hardest sections. The in-game Shop also has some cool items to pick up that can help including the Grapple Gun, Rainbow Magic Carpet, Super Coil, Speed Coil and Portal Gun. Just make sure you have enough cash to spend!

If you want to add more festive razzle-dazzle to your character, then head on over to the Escape Santa's Workshop Obby Store. Here you'll find a number of fun extra animations that can be purchased with Robux. These include The Spinner, Helicopter, Slinky, Fabulous, Transformer and Derp animation, all of which are hilarious!

CATALOG AND ROBUX

If you want to buy more items and gear for your Robloxian, head to the Avatar Shop and see what you can pick up from the Catalog. There are lots of free items to choose from, but the best swag costs Robux!

The Avatar Shop is the place to go to if you want more options for how your character looks. Browse the numerous items on display by searching for specific things or by using the category menu. There are so many items you can select that sometimes the choice can be overwhelming!

Featured Animations
Featured Faces
Featured Gear
Featured Bundles
Featured Emotes
Community Creations +
Premium +
Collectibles +
Clothing +
Body Parts +
Gear +
Accessories +
Avatar Animations +

Filters
Genre
All Genres
☐ Building
☐ Horror
☐ Town and City
☐ Military
☐ Comedy
☐ Medieval
☐ Adventure
☐ Sci-Fi
☐ Naval
☐ FPS
☐ RPG
☐ Sports
☐ Fighting
☐ Western

Korblox Deathspeaker ® 17,000
Stitchface ® 4,000
Ninja Animation Package ® 750
Violet Valkyrie ® 50,000
Oldschool Animation Pack ® 80

Toy Animation Pack ® 250
Bubbly Animation ® 250
Elemental Crystal Golem ® 400
Beautiful Hair for Beautiful People ® 95
Extreme Headphones ® 7,500

Astronaut Animation Pack ® 500
Cartoony Animation ® 250
Jester Equinox ® 250
Zombie ® 550
Bow Braids & Wispy Bangs By Beeism ® 90

Ud'zal
Err...
Old Town Road
Big Sad Eyes
Stylish Animation

You can change your avatar's face, body, arms, legs, hair, clothing and emotes as many times as you like. It's definitely worth spending some time playing around with styles and mixing and matching a variety of items. Once you're ready, hop into a game and show off your new look to your friends.

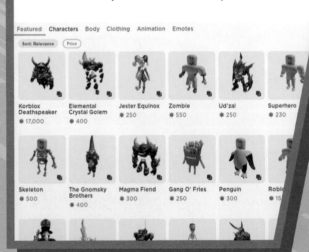

Featured | Characters | Body | Clothing | Animation | Emotes

Sort: Relevance | Price

Korblox Deathspeaker ® 17,000
Elemental Crystal Golem ® 400
Jester Equinox ® 250
Zombie ® 550
Ud'zal ® 250
Superhero ® 230

Skeleton ® 500
The Gnomsky Brothers ® 400
Magma Fiend ® 300
Gang O' Fries ® 250
Penguin ® 300
Roblo... ® 15...

Claw ed Companion ® 250

...obot
Polar Bear ® 150

Crazy Clown ® 250
Battle Ready Kenji ® 250

Beatrix the Bee
Flame Guard

Snow Gentleman
⊙ ® 400

🛠 Item Options   Ⓨ Open Details   Ⓧ Buy

Grab as many free items that you can and try them out on your avatar first to see how they look. You'll be able to get a lot of gear without paying for it, but the really interesting looking items cost Robux. Some of the paid-for stuff is cheap and some is really pricey.

Buy more in-game currency, or Robux, within the game itself using real money or pick up physical Roblox Gift Cards. Both options give you different amounts of Robux to spend in the Shop, but with the Gift Cards you can also get exclusive virtual items for your avatar!

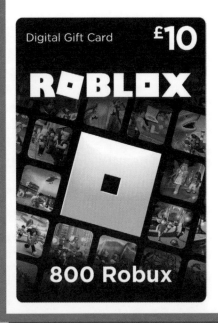

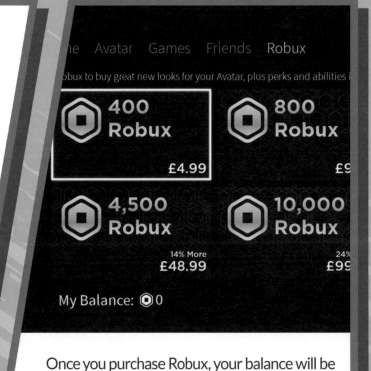

Once you purchase Robux, your balance will be shown at the top of the screen. You can then use your Robux however you like, from buying items in the Avatar Shop or for purchasing paid-for games. Once you've spent all of your Robux, you'll need to buy more and they won't last forever!

If you want to earn more Robux, try creating your own custom items and games and then selling them to other players. You'll get paid in Robux, which you can then use to buy even more items. It's worth remembering you can't get Robux for free, so watch out for any scams or links that offer them.

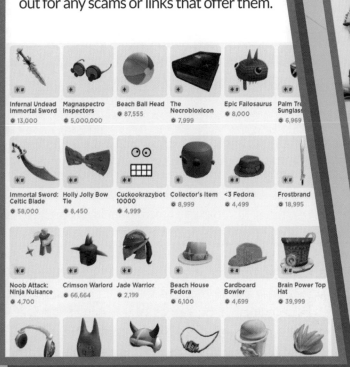

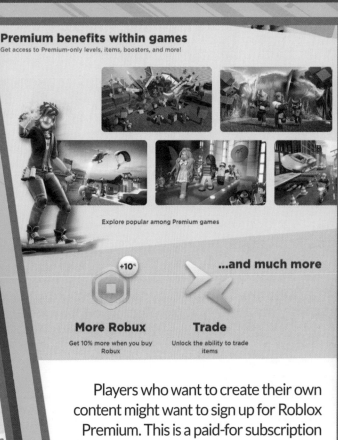

Players who want to create their own content might want to sign up for Roblox Premium. This is a paid-for subscription service that gets you a monthly Robux allowance, access to exclusive items and the ability to trade. This option is for hardcore Roblox fans only!

TOP 10 ADVENTURE GAMES

When it comes to pulse-pounding adventure games, Roblox has plenty of titles to choose from. Whether you're saving the planet or sailing the Seven Seas, there's something for everyone!

#10 THE APOCALYPSE

ROBLOX FACT: Creator Builder's Block added in super spooky maps and items for Halloween!

Creator: Builder's Block
Release Date: December 2019

When the end of the world comes, only the strongest will survive. In The Apocalypse, it's you against hordes of shuffling zombies. You'll need to team up with other survivors, hide in buildings and battle against the undead until morning comes. With limited supplies, you'll need all of your skills to last the night!

There are lots of different weapons to find and you'll need them to hold off the zombie hordes. Food and supplies are limited and need to be shared with other players. If you starve or get bitten, it's game over. If you die, you'll become a zombie and can then attack your former team mates.

#9 FLOOD ESCAPE

Creator: Crazyblox
Release Date: August 2010

ROBLOX FACT:
Hit all six buttons in the three rooms to unlock one of two special bonus rounds!

Race against time in Flood Escape to make it to safety before being swept away by rushing water. Players have to get past obstacles, solve puzzles and reach the end of each room before they drown. The game has tons of rooms and difficulty settings, so you can practice first and find the challenge that's right for you.

During its early development Flood Escape was originally just a single player game, but is now much more fun in multiplayer. Each course has three rooms to tackle, with corridors linking them together. If you're playing with others, you'll have to wait until everyone makes it to the end before you can leave the room.

ROBLOX FACT:
The Wild West VIP pack costs 10 Robux and gets you a special gun and outfit!

Creator: Starboard Studios
Release Date: September 2018

#8 THE WILD WEST

Here's your chance to explore a cowboy-themed open world that's packed with quests and action. Players can choose to be a bounty hunter, gold miner, sneaky outlaw or any number of fun Western roles. You can play solo or team up with others and form a posse to take down pesky varmints.

The latest version of the game includes new Steamboat Robbery and Fort maps, fist fights and more weapons such as the gatling gun. Starboard Studios also plans to add a Building Mode to the game in 2021, which will allow players to construct their own structures to show off to their friends.

#7 Your BiZARRE ADVENTURE

Creator: Bizarre Studios
Release Date: September 2018

This great Roblox game is actually based on the 7th longest-running Manga series, JoJo's Bizarre Adventure by Hirohiko Araki. It features a sprawling open-world to explore with other players and a deep combat system to get to grips with. You can battle mobs for rewards, take on quests and level up by using skill points.

Players can ride horses and compete against others in the Metal Ball races. If you win you'll be rewarded with lots of money and a special requiem arrow. Although the game can be a bit confusing at first, stick with it and you'll soon learn that there's more to Your Bizarre Adventure than meets the eye!

ROBLOX FACT:
Sign up to the game's VIP servers and get x2 item spawning that lasts longer!

#6 A PIRATE'S TALE

Creator: A Pirate's Tale
Release Date: March 2018

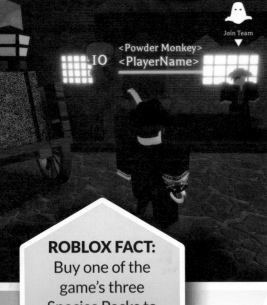

ROBLOX FACT:
Buy one of the game's three Species Packs to get all sorts of creature skins!

Get ready to sail the Seven Seas on a superb swashbuckling adventure with A Pirate's Tale. This awesome open-world game is set in the world of the Cursed Seas and players take on the role of a scurvy seadog looking for plenty of treasure. You can also customise your character at the start to make sure you have the perfect pirate look!

Players explore a huge ocean dotted with islands, ports and secrets to discover as they join one of two warring pirate factions. Undertake quests to earn lots of loot, sword fight with other pirates and battle giant sea creatures along the way. Have you got what it takes to become the most black-hearted pirate in history?

#5 APOCALYPSE RISING

ROBLOX FACT:
If you like the game, you can pay 200 Robux to unlock the sequel, Apocalypse Rising 2!

Creator: Gusmanak
Release Date: April 2008

Only the toughest will have what it takes to survive in Apocalypse Rising! This pulse-pounding open-world zombie survival game is one of the older titles on Roblox, but it's had so much cool content added to it over the years that it's still worth playing. Players can also sign up to the game's VIP servers for 100 Robux per month.

The game has one of the largest maps of any Roblox title and tons of regular players. You'll be battling it out with other survivors to take on hordes of the undead in a deserted wasteland. Work together, find supplies and weapons, fight off attacking zombies and build defences in order to live as long as possible.

#4 ADVENTURE STORY!

One of the most popular games on Roblox, Adventure Story! is a multiplayer turn-based adventure title that takes place in a fun cartoony world. Players travel the land on their own or in groups to explore strange lands, battle evil enemies and learn powerful abilities. Completing quests rewards players with treasure and relics.

Creator: vetexgames
Release Date: September 2018

Combat is unique as players take turns fighting enemies and attempting to reduce their opponent's energy. By teaming up with others it's much easier (and faster) to take down larger foes and reap the rewards. A recent Dungeon Update added all-new enemies, global leaderboards and lobbies, as well as more items, gear and powers.

ROBLOX FACT:
After an update in December 2020 vetexgames made Adventure Story! Free-to-play!

#3

HIDE AND SEEK EXTREME

ROBLOX FACT:
Additional 'It' characters can be purchased by players for Robux in the Shop!

Creator: Tim7775
Release Date: January 2015

Who'd have thought that such a simple kids' game could be turned into one of the most popular titles on Roblox? With over 1.4 billion visits, Hide and Seek Extreme has been a huge success. The basic idea is simple, with one playing being 'It' and having to find the other players hiding in a level. That's it!

Of course things aren't quite that easy, as the levels in Hide and Seek Extreme are huge and your character has been shrunk down to a tiny size. Players that are hiding get to choose all kinds of giant objects to sneak behind, but they also need to be careful they don't fall off the edges or get trapped somewhere.

Whoever is playing as 'It' is given three special abilities to help find hidden players. These include Glue, Camera, and Sprint and Stun, all of which can be combined to help you catch everyone. When the game begins it selects a random map and player to be the seeker, so no two levels are ever the same.

All players spawn into the level at the same point including the seeker. Anyone hiding then has a short amount of time to find somewhere to conceal themselves before the seeker begins looking for them. The seeker has to find everyone before the time runs out to win the game, while hiders just have to not be found!

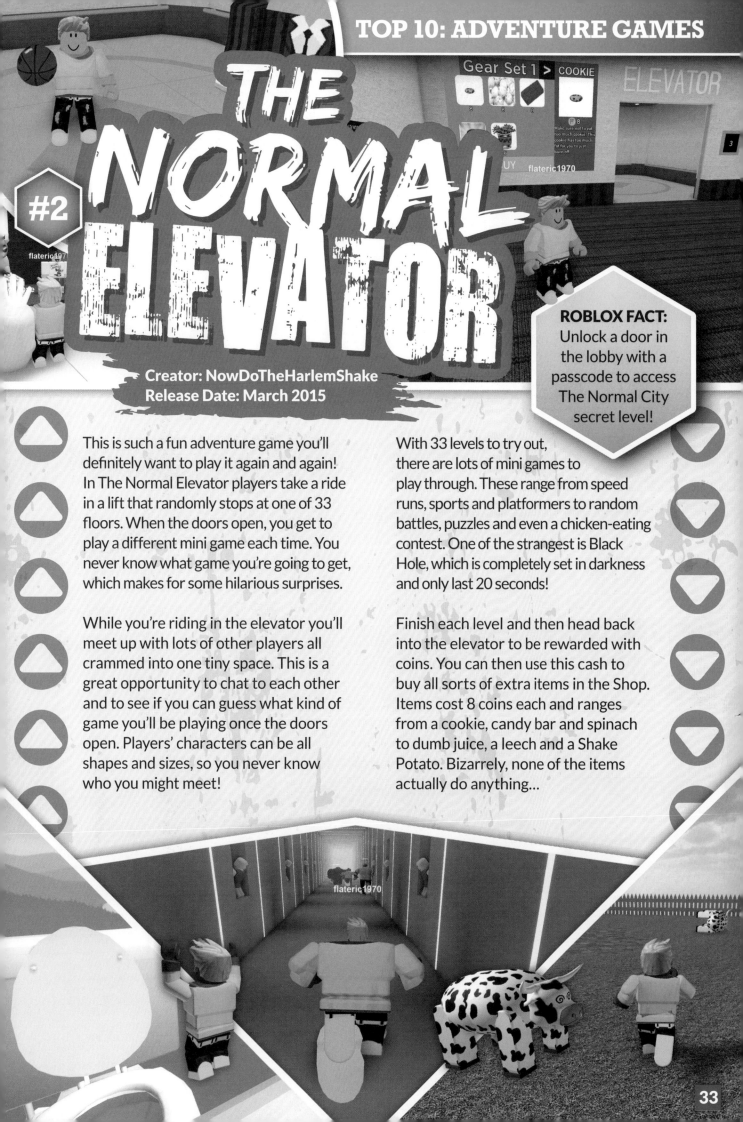

#2

THE NORMAL ELEVATOR

Creator: NowDoTheHarlemShake
Release Date: March 2015

ROBLOX FACT:
Unlock a door in the lobby with a passcode to access The Normal City secret level!

This is such a fun adventure game you'll definitely want to play it again and again! In The Normal Elevator players take a ride in a lift that randomly stops at one of 33 floors. When the doors open, you get to play a different mini game each time. You never know what game you're going to get, which makes for some hilarious surprises.

While you're riding in the elevator you'll meet up with lots of other players all crammed into one tiny space. This is a great opportunity to chat to each other and to see if you can guess what kind of game you'll be playing once the doors open. Players' characters can be all shapes and sizes, so you never know who you might meet!

With 33 levels to try out, there are lots of mini games to play through. These range from speed runs, sports and platformers to random battles, puzzles and even a chicken-eating contest. One of the strangest is Black Hole, which is completely set in darkness and only last 20 seconds!

Finish each level and then head back into the elevator to be rewarded with coins. You can then use this cash to buy all sorts of extra items in the Shop. Items cost 8 coins each and ranges from a cookie, candy bar and spinach to dumb juice, a leech and a Shake Potato. Bizarrely, none of the items actually do anything…

Creator: Sonar Studios
Release Date: July 2020

#1 Dragon Adventures

Who wants a boring pet when you can have a dragon? In this awesome adventure game, that's exactly what you can do! Gather dragon eggs, place them in the cauldron and then pick them up when they're ready to hatch. There are lots of different species to collect and each of the scaly beasts has a variety of strengths and abilities.

Once you've selected your main dragon you'll be taught how to ride and fly it, train it to breathe fire and feed your pet to keep it healthy. The more eggs that you find on your journey, the more dragon species you'll be able to add to your lair. Dragons can also level up, so stick with your chosen beast to make them powerful.

Hop on to your dragon and explore the world around you to find more eggs, battle enemies and complete challenging quests. Players can move from stage to stage by using the World Teleporter located at the centre. The more worlds that you tackle, the more adventures you'll have and the more essential items you'll collect.

You'll also have the ability to design and build your own base from a variety of materials. As you travel around the world and complete more quests, you can use your cash to purchase better building supplies. It's also possible for players to grow all kinds of different crops near the base, with which to feed their ever-growing dragons.

It's possible for up to 10 players to take part in a game of Dragon Adventures, although the worlds are so large that you might not encounter any other characters for a while.

You can choose to team up with your fellow dragon owners to take on enemies and work together or face foes on your own for a tougher challenge.

To give yourself a handy boost be sure to check out the Dragon Adventures Store. Here you'll be able to buy a number of cool Gamepasses to help you on your quests. You can pick up all sorts of extras such as a Lucky Egg, Big Backpack, Lucky Trainer and the VIP Pass which gets you whopping +100% double XP!

With over 207 million visits since the game launched, Dragon Adventures is easily one of the most popular titles on Roblox. To keep players interested there have been a number of updates added to the game including special themed events and content. Even bigger updates are promised, so keep checking back to see what's new!

ROBLOX FACT:
Players who tried out the game at Christmas got lots of festive treats!

CELEBRITY FANS

All sorts of famous faces have been popping up in Roblox recently, from musicians promoting their latest songs to Premier League football clubs. Keep your eyes peeled for more special online events happening all of the time!

WEYES BLOOD

In 2019 singer songwriter Weyes Blood released an album called *Titanic Rising*. One of the songs from her recording session was a bonus track called *Titanic Risen*. The same song now appears in the game Roblox Titanic, a sinking ship simulation, along with others!

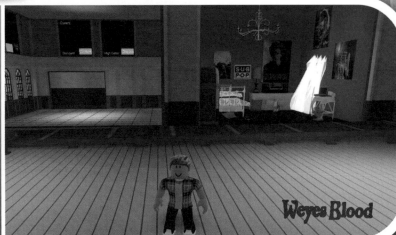

LIL NAS X

Rapper Lil Nas X hosted his own Roblox virtual live concert in November, 2020 and fans could go online and join in! The show included a motion-captured avatar of Lil Nas X performing and there were also exclusive digital items to buy with Robux.

AVA MAX

To celebrate the launch of her new album *Heaven & Hell*, pop star Ava Max held a virtual launch party in September, 2020. There was a Q&A with Ava, she performed new songs and there were even in-game events all set in a sky-high dance floor!

Liverpool FC: Firmino's Jersey
By ROBLOX ● Item Owned

This item is available in your inventory.

Price	Free
Type	Shirt
Genres	Sports
Description	Referred to as the "engine" by manager Jurgen Klopp, Roberto Firmino's work ethic is matched only by his creativity.

Try On | 3D

LIVERPOOL FC

In the summer of 2019, Liverpool FC signed a massive deal with Roblox to add their team kit into the game for a limited time. Players could pick up the 2019/20 shirt with one of 11 players' names on them plus a special bonus scarf!

PARTY PLACE

Roblox hosted its 7th Annual Bloxy Awards and the One World: Together At Home concert last year in its new Party Place venue. This virtual environment will be the location for more cool events and you never know which celebrities might appear!

TONES AND I

The music game Splash launched a special Roblox event in November, 2020 with multi-platinum selling artist Tones and I. As well as special virtual appearances from the singer, there was also a Tones and I world and mini games to play!

CELEBRITY YOUTUBERS

There are lots of YouTubers that play Roblox, but some are superstars with millions of hits. Check out gaming videos from the likes of Tofuu, DanTDM, Denis, Poke and Flamingo for some hilarious moments, handy tips and much more!

TOP 10

SPORTS GAMES

If sports games are your thing, then Roblox has you covered! From hard-hitting American football to scoring goals in the Prem, there are all sorts of competitive sports titles to try out.

#10 SUPER STRIKER LEAGUE

Creator: Cinder Studio
Release Date: June 2019

ROBLOX FACT: During the RB Battles Season 2 event, players could try a special Goalbusters mode!

Super Striker League ramps things up to the max by adding awesome power-ups, special player abilities and cool items to the beautiful game. In any match you could be playing with bomb balls, trying to score a goal with a giant boulder or zooming across the pitch at super speed.

Balls in the game are different colours and have various abilities, affecting your chances of scoring. Players can also hold down the kick button to charge up, allowing the ball to travel further and higher. Go for a Super Strike shot straight down the middle and you'll knock off 75% of the goalkeeper's stamina!

WEIGHT LIFTING SIMULATOR 5

#9

sec

Stick
flateric1970

Creator: Rumble Studios
Release Date: November 2019

x2 Strength x2 Durability

Akimbo Weights

It's time to get pumped! The aim of this game is start lifting weights to build up your muscles and grow larger. The bigger you get, the heavier the weights you can lift. Players start out quite skinny and small and can only pick up very small dumb bells. The more they pump themselves up, the musclier they'll get.

The game is hilarious as you can hear other players groaning and straining as they lift weights and try to get stronger. Fights will often break out where you're training and your character may get trashed by larger weight lifters. Train hard, collect gems and team up with other players to see how you can grow massive and be the champ!

#8 OWN A CAR AND RACE!

There are a number of games on Roblox called Own a Car and Race, but this is the one to check out. Also known as OACAR, this is a racing game that's really fun to play with your mates. Players can choose from one of nine different cars and race them on a variety of tracks. Try not to crash too much!

Creator: TrafficGames
Release Date: February 2020

Check out your chosen vehicle in your garage before taking it for a spin, take a look at cars from older versions of the game in the OACAR Museum and listen to the realistic rev of those engines. Out on the track you'll need to have your pedal to the metal to beat other drivers and see if you have what it takes to be a true racing champion.

The Original cars

ROBLOX: NBA FINALS 2020

#7

ROBLOX FACT: Head over to the Roblox: NBA Finals 2020 Store for Trails and plenty of bonus EXP!

Creator: LukeGabriel's Fan Group
Release Date: July 2019

Get ready to shoot some hoops and pull off all-star slam dunks! Basketball is one of the most popular games in the world, and this title is packed with fast-paced sports action. Practise your game first, choose a cool custom armband and then take to the court against your favourite NBA teams.

You'll need to learn how to play the game first and understand the rules. After a few sessions you'll be dribbling like a pro and scoring plenty of points. Players can also check out their game stats to see how they're doing and what areas they need to improve. Before you know it you could be the next MVP of your team!

TPS: ULTIMATE SOCCER

#6

Creator: TAYFUN7
Release Date: February 2020

If you prefer football games to be more realistic, then be sure to check out TPS: Ultimate Soccer! This simulation features a more classic version of the beautiful game for players to get to grips with, letting you join a team and battle it out to make it to the top of the league. Players can practice first or just jump into a full game.

You can also build your own Dream Team by purchasing players cards with credits. Pick the squad that works for you and mix and match players as required. Progress through matches to level up and improve your team's performance. Do you have what it takes to reach the top and dominate the league?

ROBLOX FACT: TPS: Ultimate Soccer won awards in 2012 and 2020 for being one of the best Roblox games!

#5

FOOTBALL FUSION

Creator: XSTNS GAMES
Release Date: August 2019

When it comes to quality American football games on Roblox, Football Fusion is easily one of the best. As in the real sport, two teams of competing players head out on to the field to try and beat each other in a hard-hitting, rough and tumble game of four quarters. The team with the most amount of points at the end is the winner.

Players can take on a number of essential roles such as quarterback and kicker, as they try to move the ball deeper into the opponent's half. You can practice to improve your skills first or jump straight into a standard game. Check your stats to see how you and your team are performing and even customise your jersey.

DODGEBALL!

Creator: alexnewtron
Release Date: December 2009

#4

You'll need super-fast reflexes and timing to win in Dodgeball! Based on the popular US sport, the game features two teams attempting to hit each other with balls for points. You can pass the ball to a teammate first or just throw it at an opponent to cause them damage. Once a player has been hit four times, they're out of the game.

It is possible to avoid (or dodge) balls by waiting until it turns white and then quickly moving out of the way. At the end of a round the winning team gets to show off and one of you will be crowned MVP. There are also gamepasses to purchase for Robux which can give you special balls including one shaped like a pumpkin!

DODGEBALL
WIPEOUT THE OTHER TEAM

RB2 WORLD 2

ROBLOX FACT: Players start off with 1000 Koins, but can buy more in the game's Shop!

Creator: CollegiateJokes
Release Date: June 2017

#3

Although developer CollegiateJokes has since moved on to create RB World 3, we actually think this version of the game is more solid. Created a few years ago, the game has had a number of updates that have really polished it into a special sports title. If you're looking for the best basketball game on Roblux, then this is it!

It may only be a single player game, but RB World 2 is still a fun experience with plenty for players to get to grips with. When you first start a game you'll get the opportunity to customise your player in detail. From the way your character looks and their team position to skillset and uniform, there are lots of options to try out.

Once your character is set you're best trying out your moves on the hardwood of your own private practice court. This will allow you to prepare for the tough games ahead without the distraction of other players. When you feel ready head on over to the Park, Rec. or League to try your hand at a game of basketball for real.

Take on other players in one-on-one matches to see who can score the most points. Block, duck, weave and shoot to beat your opponents and slam dunk the ball into the basket. Boost your game by heading to the Store and purchasing extras such as the Jumpshot Editor, Extra Slots, Big Gym or Intro Animations. Go check it out!

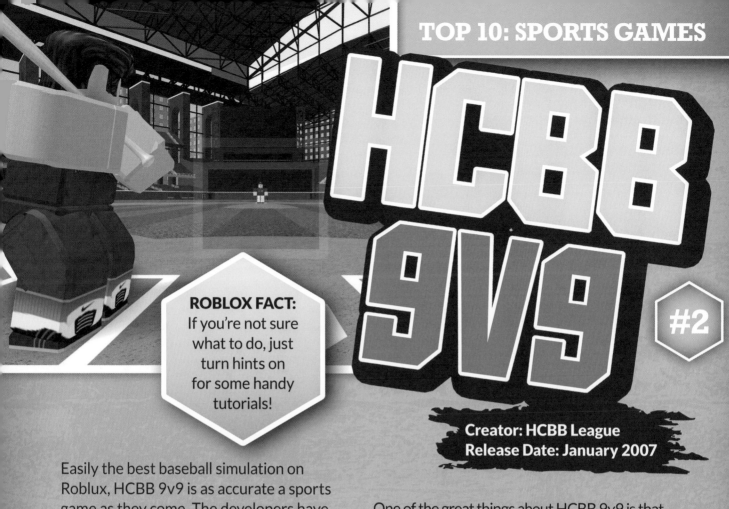

HCBB 9V9

#2

ROBLOX FACT:
If you're not sure what to do, just turn hints on for some handy tutorials!

Creator: HCBB League
Release Date: January 2007

Easily the best baseball simulation on Roblux, HCBB 9v9 is as accurate a sports game as they come. The developers have spent years fine-tuning the title and adding all sorts of essential updates, If you're a massive fan of baseball or completely new to the game, then you should definitely take a look at what this has to offer.

Start the game in the dugout and you can select from a number of handy options, Buy gear and uniforms for your player, purchase walk up, home run and strikeout songs and view animations. You can also view the progress of the current game, league stats or head on over to the batting cages to get some practice in.

One of the great things about HCBB 9v9 is that players can jump straight into a game, joining others on the pitch to bat and field for real teams. If your team is batting, you'll take your turn stepping up to the plate to take swings before dashing to bases. The fielding team can try to catch balls, make passes to teammates and get players out.

You can alter the speed at which you pitch or swing to improve your game. Additional options let players select a variety of ballparks and real teams to join. Select a batting cage server and take part on a Home Run Derby to see how good you are. Whether you're playing a quick game or working up through the leagues, HCBB 9v9 has it all!

#1 KICK OFF

Brazil Wins!

ROBLOX FACT:
There's a 0.2% chance of you earning the elusive 1000 Goals badge in the game!

Creator: CM Games
Release Date: November 2015

Although this game was created over five years ago it's still easily the best football simulation title on Roblox. With over a massive 250 million visits since its launch, there's no doubting its popularity. Over time creator CM Games has tweaked and fine-tuned the game's content, making it a smash hit with players worldwide.

Up to eight players can take part in matches for some full-on footie action. If you want to play in your own game with just your friends then you can always pay 100 Robux and grab a Private Server. This will allow you to set up a match exactly how you like and you won't get random players dropping in for a kickabout.

As soon as you start the game you're dropped into a match that can take place on a real pitch or even a Halloween stadium. Teams are made up of five players each including a CPU-controlled goalkeeper and matches are short but fast-paced. Once a match ends, there's a short intermission where you get to kick around a giant football!

Your player has a number of skills that they can use to help them score goals. These are Power, Trickshot and Stamina. Boost up the pitch to chase the ball, tackle other players and try to smash a volley into the back of the net. Scoring is quote easy, but getting hold of the ball and keeping possession of it can be tricky.

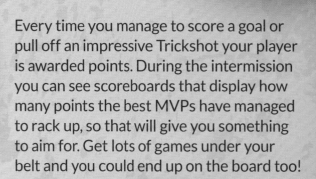

Every time you manage to score a goal or pull off an impressive Trickshot your player is awarded points. During the intermission you can see scoreboards that display how many points the best MVPs have managed to rack up, so that will give you something to aim for. Get lots of games under your belt and you could end up on the board too!

When you manage to score a goal, the distance that you took the shot from is displayed and your character will do a cool victory pose. Although you can play in a real-life team, it's not possible to select which one you'll join at the start of a game. However, you will get to wear that squad's kit and get your name on the back of your shirt.

The game's Store has some additional items that you might want to buy with Robux. These can really enhance your game and help give you an edge over other players. Up for grabs are extra Stamina, x2 Credits, a Power boost and faster Trickshots. With all of these added to your skills, you'll be unstoppable on the pitch!

DID YOU KNOW?

So you think you know everything there is to know about Roblox? Well think again! There are all sorts of amazing facts, stats and tips hidden away inside your favourite game. Here's a selection of them to amaze and impress your mates.

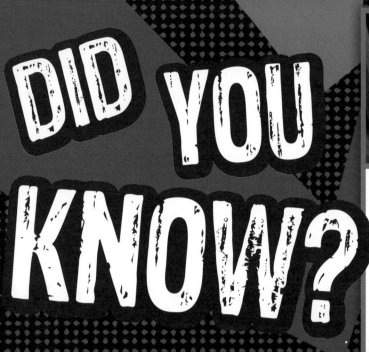

The game wasn't always called Roblox! When the platform was first being developed, one of the names being considered for it was DynaBlocks. The other possible name was GoBlocks, but everyone agreed Roblox was easier to remember!

In MeepCity it's actually possible to find a secret entrance to the teacher's lounge. Go through the cafeteria and down the stairs to the basement. Climb into the vent on the wall and follow it all the way through to the lounge!

A couple of times a year Roblox sets a design challenge for its players. In 2020 fans had to create a Roblox gift card design and 12 talented winners each received a $100 gift card to spend in the game. Next time that winner could be you!

When you first spawn in to the Make a Cake game, head over to the Special Batter selections and walk all the way up the conveyor belt to the ladder. Go through the flaming logs to discover a secret room with a giant cake inside.

Whenever a character dies in Roblox, the sound they usually make is either 'Oof' or 'Uuhhh'. This strange sound effect has been in the game since it first launched and has also been used in lots of funny memes, videos and even the Roblox game, Oof!

Did you know there are two secret languages in the game Welcome to Bloxburg? When you spawn in, press Options and use the menu to select either Oofish or Robonese. Do that and then everyone will speak complete gibberish!

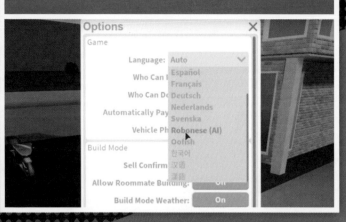

When it comes to big numbers, Roblox has many other games beat. Over 36 million players in 40 countries log on to Roblox every day, clocking up 1.5 billion hours of game play. There are also over 7 million creators making cool content.

Instead of trying to escape in the game Jailbreak, head outside and find the sewer grate. Go inside and follow a path on the right to discover four tiny turtles and a pizza box. This is a sneaky reference to the Teenage Mutant Ninja Turtles!

Over 600,000 fans and over four million players watched the 7th Annual Bloxy Awards in 2020. The top prizes were won by Adopt Me!, Arsenal, Dungeon Quest, Adventure Up and Super Striker League. Who will win awards in 2021?

This secret in Work at a Pizza Place is easy and well worth checking out. When you first spawn into the game, go round the side of the pizza restaurant and jump through a dark patch on the wall to discover your own private hideout!

STAYING SAFE, BEING SOCIAL

FOR PLAYERS

PICKING A USERNAME
NEVER choose a username that has your personal information, such as your real name or birthday.

STAY SECRET
Don't ever give out your real name, address, phone number, or the school you go to. Roblox will never need this info, and neither will anyone else. Roblox has chat software that will automatically try to filter out real-life names for a reason.

STAY IN-GAME
Scammers may ask you to trade money or items outside of the game. That's a good way to lose things. The trading menu in Roblox is designed to protect you, so stick to that and never give anything to people outside the game, no matter how trustworthy they may appear.

DON'T BE AFRAID TO REPORT
Players can easily mute and report inappropriate or abusive chat message, or disturbing content. Just use the Report Abuse system that's located on every single menu and Roblox will be notified and take action as soon as possible.

TELL YOUR PARENTS
Be brave. If someone is bothering you or you saw something you didn't like, tell a parent or guardian. Don't be afraid to say if someone is being inappropriate on Roblox. This game is for everyone and no one should be made to feel unsafe!

"I HEARD ABOUT A ROBUX GENERATOR!"
There are no such thing as Robux Generators – they're made up by scammers to steal money and accounts from players. Don't fall for it. Never trust any websites that aren't official. All official websites end with '.roblox.com'.

FOR PARENTS

BE INVOLVED
The best thing parents can do to make sure their children stay safe playing Roblox is to simply talk to them about the dangers. Make an account for yourself as you make one for your child. You'll even be able to add them as your child on Roblox, allowing you to ensure the social aspects of the game aren't getting in the way of them having fun.

"MY KID IS BEING BULLIED"
If someone is bothering your child, you should report and block them. By clicking on a username you can easily block a user and prevent them from ever contacting your child. By reporting abuse you can make sure that Roblox is aware of the situation.

SAFETY FEATURES
You can sign into your child's account and choose the level of privacy that they have. Make sure you choose the correct date of birth for your child as it sets the default security settings depending on how old they are. You can further modify the settings so that no one can contact your child, or that everyone can. Older players have more options.

MESSAGES AND CHAT
You can easily view your child's private message and chat histories from the main screen. You can also see your child's online friends, the games they've made, and anything they've purchased. If anything looks off, you can then take action.

PROTECTING YOUNGER CHILDREN
While Roblox is tamer than most games, some games feature violence or scary situations. You can go to the Account Restrictions section of your child's account to restrict them from playing anything too intense for their age group.

For many more resources we recommend going to Roblox's official parent's guide at: www.corp.roblox.com/parents There you'll find tutorials for navigating the platform, as well as tips for online safety.